# A Day With
# HOMO ERECTUS

## LIFE 400,000 YEARS AGO

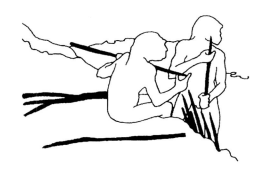

DR. FIORENZO FACCHINI

# A Day With
# HOMO ERECTUS

## LIFE 400,000
## YEARS AGO

*Illustrations by*
GIORGIO BACCHIN

TWENTY-FIRST CENTURY BOOKS / BROOKFIELD, CONNECTICUT

*English translation copyright © 2003 by Twenty-First Century Books*
*Originally published by Editoriale Jaca Book spa*
*Via Gioberti 7,*
*20123, Milano, Italy*
*www.jacabook.it*

*Library of Congress Cataloging-in-Publication Data*
*Facchini, Fiorenzo, 1929–*
*[Fiorenzo Facchini racconta la giornata di un Homo erectus. English]*
*A day with Homo erectus : life 400,000 years ago / Fiorenzo Facchini; illustrations by Giorgio Bacchin.*
*p. cm. — (Early humans)*
*Translation of: Fiorenzo Facchini racconta la giornata di un Homo erectus.*
*Includes index.*
*ISBN 0-7613-2766-5 (lib. bdg.)*
*1. Homo erectus—Juvenile literature. I. Bacchin, Giorgio. II. Title. III. Series.*

*GN284 .F3313 2003*
*569.9—dc21      2002015007*

*Published by Twenty-First Century Books*
*A Division of The Millbrook Press, Inc.*
*2 Old New Milford Road*
*Brookfield, Connecticut 06804*
*www.millbrookpress.com*

*Printed in Italy*
*2 4 5 3 1*

# CONTENTS

# FOREWORD

In the first volume of this series, *Homo habilis,* arrows point to pictures which are far, in time and space, from the protagonist's story. We will also see arrows in this volume, where *Homo erectus* is the main character.

The arrows point to objects that will become part of the future cultural history of humankind. We will see significant signs of thought and projection of thought in *Homo erectus,* much more than we saw in the story of *Homo habilis.*

When *Homo erectus* appeared, he already had the ability to speak. He also had a greater capacity than *Homo habilis* to convey to others, by way of teaching and sharing his own experiences, a whole spectrum of knowledge relating to himself, others, and the world around him.

Insofar as works of art and handmade tools convey the human abilities already existing in remote epochs, we can understand how thoughts, language, and society have always played overlapping roles in the human adventure. Thus biological and cultural dimensions come together in one unified vision of the prehistoric human being. We can detect many cultural elements of the Paleolithic age (for example: a system of symbols, rituals, art, counting, techniques for production), which will be even more apparent in Neolithic age.

# INTRODUCTION

## ENTERING THE WORLD OF
## *HOMO ERECTUS*

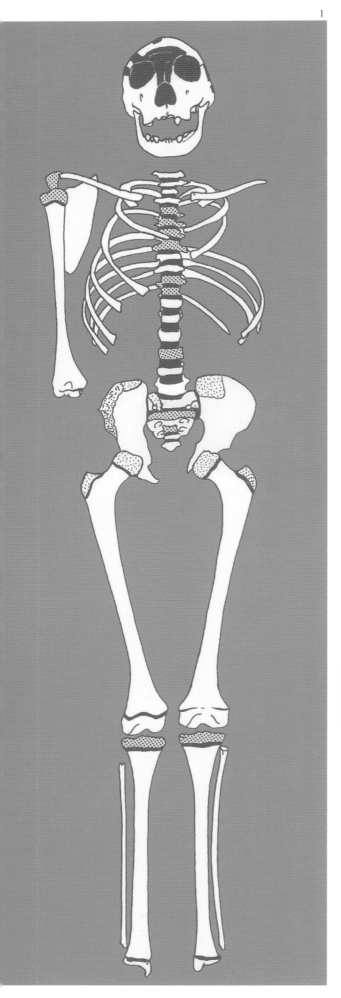

# INTRODUCTION

The name *Homo erectus* refers to a group of humans that lived between 1.6 million and 150,000—100,000 years ago.

The word "erectus" does not really have a literal meaning here because *Homo habilis* also had erect posture and practiced bipedalism. The name comes from various remains that were found on the island of Java at the end of the nineteenth century.

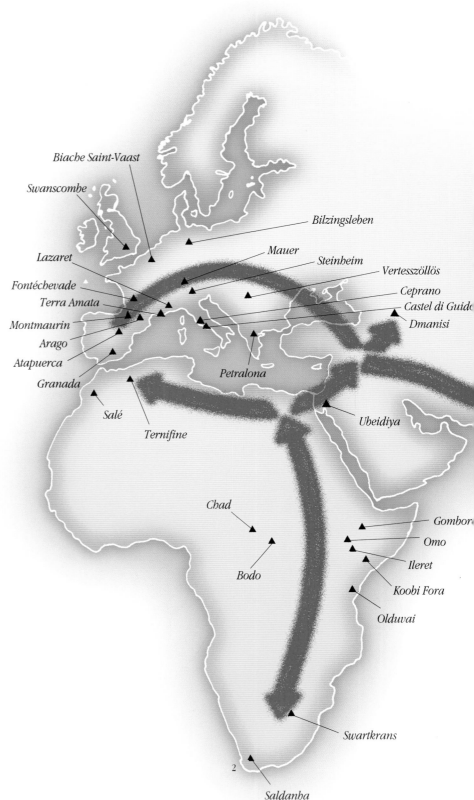

Biache Saint-Vaast
Swanscombe
Bilzingsleben
Lazaret
Mauer
Steinheim
Vertesszöllös
Fontéchevade
Ceprano
Terra Amata
Castel di Guido
Montmaurin
Dmanisi
Arago
Atapuerca
Petralona
Granada
Salé
Ubeidiya
Ternifine
Chad
Gombor
Omo
Bodo
Ileret
Koobi Fora
Olduvai
Swartkrans
Saldanha

These were referred to as the *Pithecanthropus erectus* ("monkey-man who walks upright") who lived in various epochs during the Pleistocene period.

Remains of *Homo erectus* were also found in Asia and in Europe, but *Homo erectus* came from Africa, where he would have evolved from the family tree of *Homo habilis* somewhere about 1.6 million years ago. Various remains were found in the area around Lake Turkana (Kenya), in Ethiopia, and in Tanzania. The earliest African specimens of *Homo erectus* are called *Homo ergaster*. From eastern Africa, *Homo erectus* would have migrated to southern Africa and northern Africa (Algeria, Morocco).

The migration of *Homo erectus* to Europe and Asia must have taken place more than 1 million years ago. Remains of *Homo erectus* dating back from 1.6 million years ago were found in Dmanisi, Georgia (in the former Soviet Union.) In Spain, the archaeological site of Atapuerca has produced numerous skeletal remains that can be dated from 800,000 years ago. *Homo erectus* was present in Ceprano, Lazio (Italy), 800,000 years ago. Various sites in Europe, such as Tautavel, Mauer, Petralona, Terra Amata, Steinheim, Swanscombe, Verstesszöllös, Bilzingsleben, and Isernia, among others, have also revealed remains from subsequent eras.

*1.* In Koobi Fora (Kenya) a skeleton of Homo ergaster/erectus *dating from about 1.6 million years ago was found. Here we see a restoration: the missing parts of the specimen are solid brown; the lightly dotted areas are the parts that were filled in based on what is on the other side; the darker dotted areas indicate parts that were added to complete the picture.*

*2.* On the map, we see important sites where remains of Homo erectus *have been found and the routes he took when he left Africa and populated Europe and Asia.*

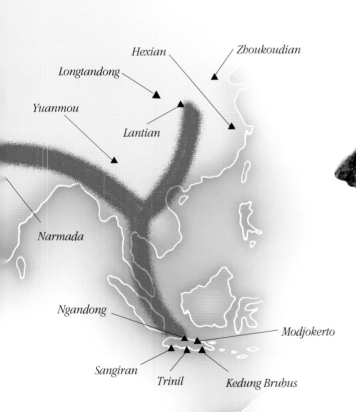

Hexian

Zhoukoudian

Longtandong

Yuanmou

Lantian

Narmada

Ngandong

Modjokerto

Sangiran

Trinil

Kedung Brubus

*3. Also from Koobi Fora (Kenya) another skull of* Homo ergaster/erectus. *This one also dates from 1.6 million years ago. Its cranial capacity measures 49 cubic inches (800 cc).*

3

**1.** *Restored skull of the so-called Peking Man (Sinanthropus pekinensis), discovered in Zhoukoudian, about 25 miles (40 kilometers) from the capital of China. Over the years, scientists have found many interesting remains in this area.*

**2.** *A drawing that shows how humans who lived in Zhoukoudian cave might have looked. They are called* Homo erectus *of China.*

**3. – 4.** *Dragon's Teeth Hill, the mountain where Peking Man lived in a big cave. In the upper drawing, we see how wide the cave was before the upper part of it collapsed, about 300,000 years ago. The inhabitants were still able to use the space, although it had become much smaller. The second drawing shows the changes.*

*Some carved stones that were found at Zhoukoudian:*
**5.** *A point of an arrow.*
**6.** *A chopping tool.*
**7.** *A discoidal chopper.*

Remains from the island of Java, found at different geological layers, have shed light on the various forms of *Pithecanthropus* that lived in several epochs during the Pleistocene period (between a little more than 1 million and 100,000 years ago). These specimens show morphological resemblances and an evolution toward an increasing cerebralization. Apart from those on Java, remains of *Homo erectus* have been found in Zhoukoudian, Lantian, Longtandong, Jinniushan (China), and Narmada (India). The well-known remains of *Sinanthropus pekinensis* (*Homo erectus*) that were found in the cave of Zhoukoudian are similar to those of *Pithecanthropus* and date from 450,000 to 230,000 years ago.

No remains of *Homo erectus* have been found in Australia or the Americas.

8

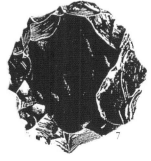

7

*8. A mountainous passage as seen from a point on the Great Wall of China, a few miles from Peking. This might have been one of the routes that* Homo erectus *of China traveled.*

**1.** *A skull of* Homo erectus *found in the cave of Arago in the eastern Pyrenees, in the territory of Tautavel, a small town not far from Perpignan (France). Tautavel Man lived inside this cave in various periods between 550,000 and 400,000 years ago. Remains that have been found indicate that he was a hunter.*

The structure of *Homo erectus* is massive and robust compared with that of *Homo habilis*. Typical *Homo erectus* features were a large, forwardly projecting browridge (supraorbital *torus*), a protrusion in the occipital bone (occipital *torus*), and a low, receding frontal bone. His face was fairly prominent (prognathe) and wide, his lower jaw (mandible) had no chin, his teeth were rather large. The cranial capacity of the earliest specimens is 55–61 cubic inches (900–1,000 cc), increasing to 73–79 cubic inches (1,200–1,300 cc) in the latest ones.

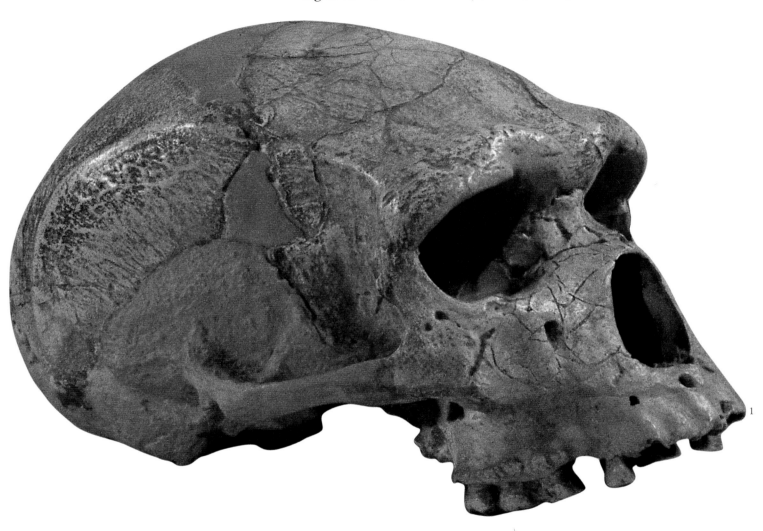

**2.** *In an environment that, at the time of Tautavel Man, was abundant with large animals, groups of hunters set up camps in rock shelters or caves and hunted freely. In this sketch, we see how the plain of Arago looked when it was dominated by a species of horses called Mosbach (*Equus caballus mosbachensis*). An opening halfway up the hill indicates a special place from which hunters could observe life on the plain and the movements of herds of bison, horses, rhinoceroses, and elephants.*

*Homo erectus* stood about 63 to 67 inches (160 to 170 centimeters) tall.

*Homo erectus* specimens from Europe and Asia are similar to those from Africa, but with some variation. Facial skeletons from the European remains show a tendency toward those traits that will be typical of the Neanderthal Man: prominent and wide face, enlargement of the braincase from front to back. The remains of *Homo erectus* of Java and China show a browridge that is flat and bladelike. In *Sinanthropus* and in other remains found in China, the upper canine teeth are spatulate.

The environment in which *Homo erectus* developed was savanna or grassland, and since he was drawn to places where the climate was mostly temperate, but with a cold season, he had to find shelter in caves

for at least some part of the year. He never stayed in one place for long, but moved around according to the availability of resources offered by the environment. The harshness of winter and the extended periods of snow and ice in the mountainous regions suggest that *Homo erectus* may have moved to a more favorable climate during the cold season. For protection from the cold, he probably wore and used animal skins.

Hunting and gathering were the way of life of *Homo erectus*. He lived in small groups of one or more families. He hunted large mammals such as bison, deer, elephant, hippopotamus, and rhinoceros, and to this end used traps, pursuing the animals with large sticks and driving them toward swamps or cliffs. The hunt was organized by the group, and the hunters sometimes had to leave the family camp and set up another campsite elsewhere, just for hunting.

The family camp had to be close to a water source and caves. The huts, which were made with branches, were outfitted with animal skins. The camp had to be close to places that could fur-

1

*1. A flake made by* Homo erectus *using the Levallois technique. Its shape was not accidental; rather, it was produced deliberately by the stone carver. Before starting to chip, the stone carver prepared a nucleus of stone, whose shape determined the final shape of the tool.*

**2.** *A drawing showing the final stages of the hippopotamus hunt.* Homo erectus *would trap large prey in the swamp and then beat them to death.*

nish raw material (notably flint) for making tools. Toolmaking was a continuation of the *Homo habilis* tradition of pebble industry (choppers and chopping tools). *Homo erectus* developed bifaces, tools which were obtained from a core of stone that was flaked on both faces and along the edges. In this we see the concept of symmetry, which does not appear to be related to the tool's function but adds to its beauty. Another type of stonework is represented in the Levallois technique, which consists of the preparation of a flake that is carved from a nucleus of stone by carefully chipping around its edges. With the passage of time, humans refined this technique so that one nucleus of stone could yield more flakes.

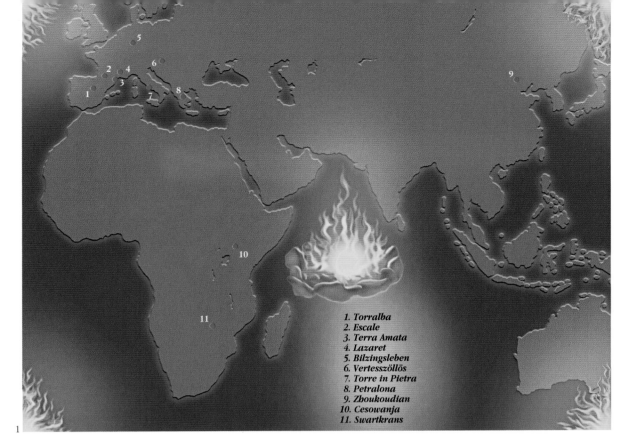

1. Torralba
2. Escale
3. Terra Amata
4. Lazaret
5. Bilzingsleben
6. Vertesszöllös
7. Torre in Pietra
8. Petralona
9. Zhoukoudian
10. Cesowanja
11. Swartkrans

**1.** *The map shows the main sites where evidence has indicated that ancient humans learned to use fire before 100,000 years ago.*

*2. – 4. The arrow points from the torch that Homo erectus is holding to two scenarios in which mastery of fire was important to human cultural development. The first picture shows the tips of two torches dating from the Neolithic age. They were found in an underground cave at Niaux, Ariège (France), whose walls had been painted in prehistoric times. Fire provided a source of light to the ancient artists who left their artwork on the walls of the cave. These caves could not have received any natural light. The next picture shows two pieces of ceramic from Mesopotamia (about 6000 B.C.E.). The paintings show deer, which symbolize the company of living beings. Ceramic work was a typical product of later humans in agricultural and sedentary (non-nomadic) societies. Fire was used in ceramic work, making it a long-lasting vehicle for passing on cultural information.*

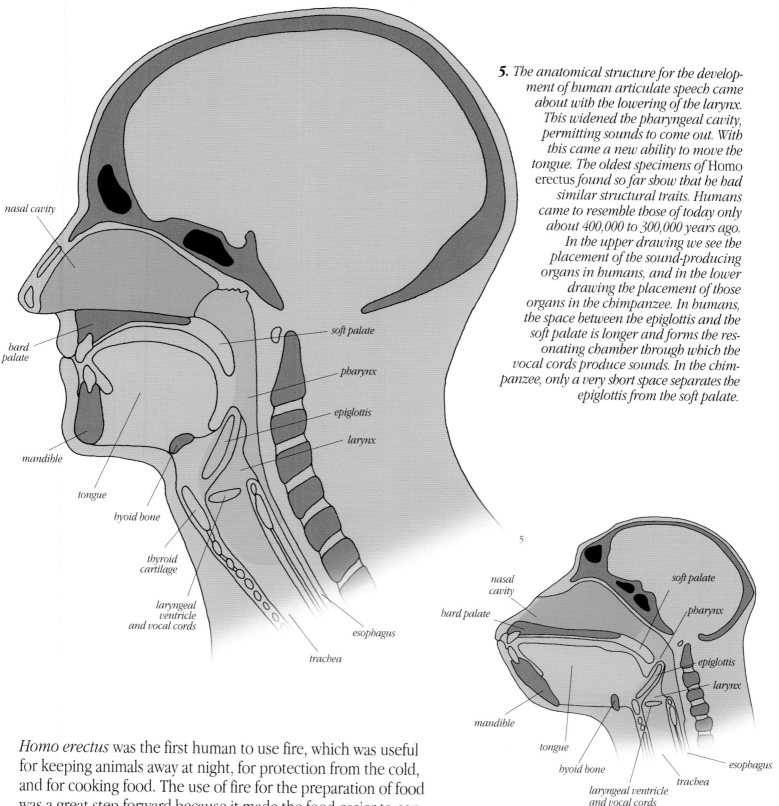

*nasal cavity*

*hard palate*

*mandible*

*tongue*

*hyoid bone*

*thyroid cartilage*

*laryngeal ventricle and vocal cords*

*soft palate*

*pharynx*

*epiglottis*

*larynx*

*esophagus*

*trachea*

**5.** *The anatomical structure for the development of human articulate speech came about with the lowering of the larynx. This widened the pharyngeal cavity, permitting sounds to come out. With this came a new ability to move the tongue. The oldest specimens of* Homo erectus *found so far show that he had similar structural traits. Humans came to resemble those of today only about 400,000 to 300,000 years ago. In the upper drawing we see the placement of the sound-producing organs in humans, and in the lower drawing the placement of those organs in the chimpanzee. In humans, the space between the epiglottis and the soft palate is longer and forms the resonating chamber through which the vocal cords produce sounds. In the chimpanzee, only a very short space separates the epiglottis from the soft palate.*

*nasal cavity*

*hard palate*

*mandible*

*tongue*

*hyoid bone*

*laryngeal ventricle and vocal cords*

*soft palate*

*pharynx*

*epiglottis*

*larynx*

*esophagus*

*trachea*

*Homo erectus* was the first human to use fire, which was useful for keeping animals away at night, for protection from the cold, and for cooking food. The use of fire for the preparation of food was a great step forward because it made the food easier to consume.

Certainly *Homo erectus* had other ways of expressing himself apart from those we recognize in his tool making and in his ability to organize his territory. His choice of suitable living space was determined by his observation of the sky and by the seasons.

His thoughts on life and death must have engaged his ability to imagine. In the cave of Zhoukoudian, fractured skulls have been found. They may be the product of special rites or ritual cannibalism. The skulls might also have been brought there for some ceremonial purpose.

# A Day
# With Kim

# HUNTING TERRITORY

We are in Kim's hut, which is on a small campsite set up at the foot of a hill in preparation for the hunt. There are no women or children, only grown men and young boys. The women and children have stayed behind at the family camp.

Hunting for large animals can be done only as a group. Kim, with his great experience, is considered the chief. He and the other men left their homes a few days ago and have camped out in a place where they know the animals will be passing by. They expect that it will be easy to catch them.

Kim is sure that bison and deer will come this way. But how will the men catch them? They will have to drive them into a nearby swamp, which Kim located when he scouted out the area. The swamp is in a valley that is connected to a narrow passageway. After the men coax the animals into the passageway and then into the swamp, they will attack them with spears and stones. This is how they trap and kill animals.

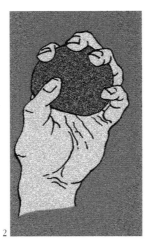

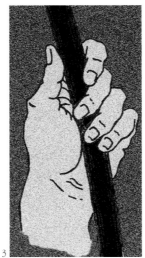

*1. The drawing shows a special kind of trap. In China, around 300,000 years ago, humans used fire and pointed spears to chase goats off rocky cliffs. They then killed and butchered them.*

*2. For hunting, humans needed to be able to grip objects. Here we see how a stone is held firmly in the hand.*

*3. When a large stick is gripped in a particular way, it can be launched in a precise direction.*

**4.** *In the Ambrona River Valley, Castilla (Spain), two sites that are close together, Ambrona and Torralba, have revealed remains that provide information about* Homo erectus's *hunting routines. The drawing shows the valley, the tracks of large mammals, and the hunters' temporary campgrounds, which were set up as close as possible to the flint quarries.*

**5.** *One of the areas in Torralba that has been excavated. It would seem that this area was used for butchering animals, because elephant remains, as well as many stone tools, have been found there.*

1. Harvesting wild fruits was just as important as hunting. It helped to develop an awareness among humans of the richness of nature. The drawing shows some blackberries (Rubus fruticosus).

2. Layers on rock formations. Homo erectus learned to evaluate the texture and hardness of stones that he found on his terrain.

3. In this drawing of a wooded area, we can see two tools that were important to Homo erectus for hunting: a hand ax and a point. These tools were found in China (Zhoukoudian, Peking).

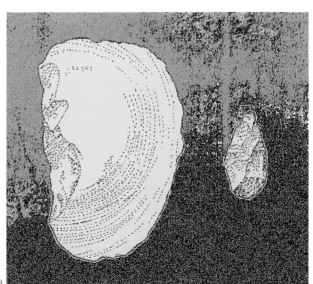

# PREPARING FOR THE HUNT

It is early morning. During their breakfast of dried meat and wild fruits, the men prepare for the hunt. This is an important time, not just because the group is together but also because Kim will give the last important instructions.

The men have taken spears with them, but they have left at the family camp the stone weapons, too heavy to be transported. They will need sticks and will have to carve stones to make hunting tools. The strong sticks will be used for beating the animals. The men find branches in the forest and carve them to make pointed spears.

For carving stones, they use blocks of flint, which they have chipped from nearby rocks. Kim suggests that they use large stones for beating the animals. They also need smaller, finer tools with sharp points, which they will stick on the end of wooden spears. These are what they will use to butcher the killed animals.

*1.* *A skull of Bison priscus, an animal that lived in France at the same time* Homo erectus. Bison *populated Europe for a long time. They were so impres-sive to humans that they were often chosen as subjects for Paleolithic paint-ings on cave walls, many of which were made by* Homo sapiens *20,000 to 15,000 years ago. The arrow to the right is pointing to some examples of the*

## BIG GAME

A small herd of bison is coming close. Kim gives the orders: "Try to goad them through the narrowest passage, toward the swamp."

Some men lurk near the passage that leads to the swamp, and others get ready to surround the herd. They pursue the bison with spears and stones, driving them into the swamp.

Some bison become stuck in the mud and try to free themselves. Using a large, knobby stick, Kim strikes the head of one of them, stunning it. Then the bison is beat-en with the stones and spears. The men do this to two other bison while the rest of the herd manage to escape.

Now it is time to cut up the captured animals and bring the pieces back to the family camp. It's not easy to make an opening in the bison's thick skin, but with the help of sharp hand axes and knives, they succeed. The smaller pieces of bison meat can be carried on the men's shoulders, and the larger ones are hung from poles that form a kind of stretcher.

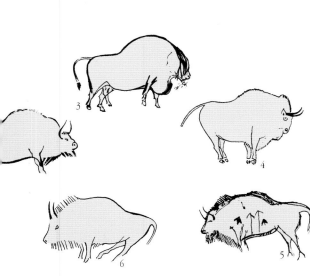

**2.** A bison at Le Portel (France). **3.** Another bison at San Román de Cardona (Spain). **4.** At Altamira (Spain). **5.** At Niaux (France). **6.** At Montespan (France). **7.** In the Volp caves (Ariège, France), a painting of a sequence of bison seems to evoke a ritual connected with hunting. A creature that is part human and part bison is striking the bow. In the center is an animal that is half deer and half bison. Finally, there is a deer with a spotted pelt.

**1.** Plan of a hut at Melka Kunturé (Ethiopia), dating from 1.4 million years ago. In the drawing: remains left by humans. Those that are colored red are horn, animal teeth, bones; those that are striped are stone tools; yellow indicates hand-held stones.

**2.** To the right of the arrow: a rock painting dating from around 3000 B.C.E., found in central Arabia, showing people returning from the hunt.

After a few hours' walk, the men reach the family camp, where they are welcomed by all. That afternoon, there is a great feast. Kim and the other men embrace their wives and children. Then they tell them about everything that has happened while they were far away on the bison hunt. But Kim's wife, Kola, also has something to tell.

When the women went on their expedition around the encampment in search of berries, roots, fruits, and small branches to make a fire, they came upon a herd of deer that were drinking from a stream. What a shame that the women were not equipped to catch any of them. Perhaps the deer are not far off now.

In the meantime, the boys had found themselves a hiding place from which they could watch small animals, like hares and marmots, passing by. They have seen these animals creep in and out of their own hiding places.

"It will not be easy to catch them," says Kim, "because marmots dig little tunnels in the ground that connect to each other, so they can always get away from hunters."

*3. Some woodland rodents that* Homo erectus *might have been familiar with: above,* Pitymis; *to the right,* Microtus; *to the left,* Clethrionomys.

**1.** *Apart from providing shelter, gorges and ravines represented access to a hidden, subterranean world. One can imagine that in ancient times these must have been sources of curiosity to humans. The photo shows the entrance of the cave of Monte Castillo in Spain. Its wall paintings suggest that this was a special place, highly respected by the prehistoric people who visited it in different epochs.*

## PRESERVING A SKULL

Kim and the others are still speaking when a boy arrives carrying a human skull. He says that he found it near a cave. Some other bones also were there. Kim takes the skull in his hand, holding it with great respect. Then he turns to the boys and says: "When we die, our life on earth ends, but something of us continues. The body is left behind, and in a short time the flesh dissolves, but some of the more durable parts remain. The skull is the part of the body that reminds us the most of the deceased who has now found a new life. This is why we keep the skull in the cave. It is our way of making sure we have the friendship and protection of the one who has left us."

Then Kim takes the skull and brings it into the cave. He sets it in a little alcove where it will be preserved for as long as the group lives in this place. They can always find it here if they wish.

**2.** *A fossilized skull of* Homo erectus *found in Steinheim, Germany. In the course of human history, the skull has always played a role in rituals that involve coming face-to-face with death. The arrow points to some examples of elaborately decorated skulls from recent time periods.*

**3.** *A skull found in the cave of Caviglione, at Grimaldi (Principality of Monaco), dating from about 20,000 years ago. It wears a headdress made of shells, and it might have been used for a fertility rite.*

**4.** *A skull from the Neolithic city of Jericho, covered in painted stucco. Shells have been placed where the eyes would be.*

**5.** *A human skull, from sometime between the ninth and fifteenth centuries* C.E., *decorated in turquoise mosaics with shells placed in the eye sockets and nasal cavity. Mixtec pre-columbian culture, Mexico.*

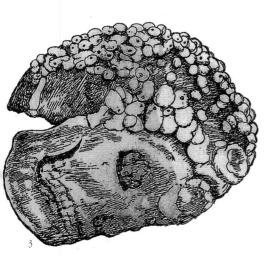

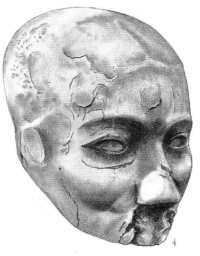

3

4

5

# THE FAMILY CAMP

We are now in Kim's camp, which is made up of different families. Some of the huts are built next to natural caves that open up on hillsides. A short distance away, a rock shelter has been transformed into a workshop for making tools from flint. The rock that supplies the raw material for the tools is close by on the side of the hill.

The cave also provides shelter in bad weather.

The place where the camp has been set up is somewhat elevated above the valley that runs between the hills. It is the perfect place for observing the movements of the herds of large mammals that go back and forth to the valley in search of water. On the side of the hill, a little stream supplies water for the group.

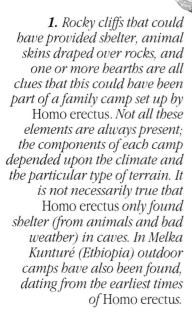

**1.** *Rocky cliffs that could have provided shelter, animal skins draped over rocks, and one or more hearths are all clues that this could have been part of a family camp set up by* Homo erectus. *Not all these elements are always present; the components of each camp depended upon the climate and the particular type of terrain. It is not necessarily true that* Homo erectus *only found shelter (from animals and bad weather) in caves. In Melka Kunturé (Ethiopia) outdoor camps have also been found, dating from the earliest times of* Homo erectus.

**2.** *A valley of the foothills of the Alps on the French-Italian border, an area rich in prehistoric remains. This photo shows what might have been a typical territory in which* Homo erectus *lived. A living area would have to have offered a broad enough view so that humans could keep track of the whereabouts of animals. It would also have to have provided a rich supply of flint, wood, and wild, edible vegetation.*

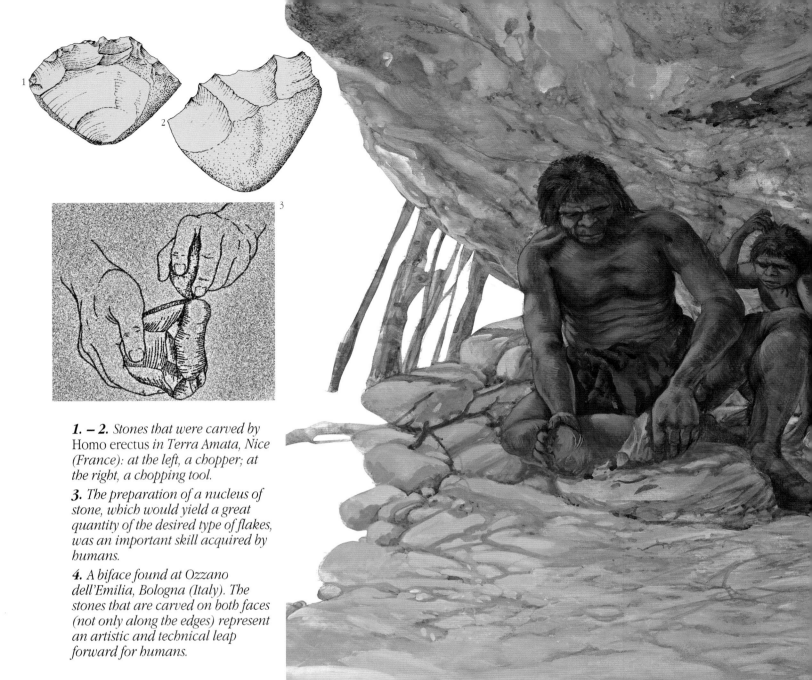

**1. – 2.** *Stones that were carved by Homo erectus in Terra Amata, Nice (France): at the left, a chopper; at the right, a chopping tool.*

**3.** *The preparation of a nucleus of stone, which would yield a great quantity of the desired type of flakes, was an important skill acquired by humans.*

**4.** *A biface found at Ozzano dell'Emilia, Bologna (Italy). The stones that are carved on both faces (not only along the edges) represent an artistic and technical leap forward for humans.*

## A LITTLE WORKSHOP

Some adults and boys are splintering rocks in the little workshop near their source of raw material for tools. They have learned the technique for splintering rocks (choppers and chopping tools) and have also learned how to obtain bifaces. By removing flakes along the edges of a stone core, they can make sharp tools that can be used to easily cut and make incisions. If flakes are removed on both faces of the core and the edges are retouched, the tool will be slimmer and more elegant. To do this, Kim suggests that they use a softer hammer, one made of deer antler or wood.

But there is another technique that Kim wants to teach the boys. He takes a nucleus of stone in his hand and begins to splinter it on one side, shaping it around the edge. He emphasizes that this technique allows you to determine the shape of the flake. It is a very valuable technique because, even if the final product is not a success, the toolmakers can minimize the amount of stone that is wasted. In this way, many other flakes can be made from the same nucleus.

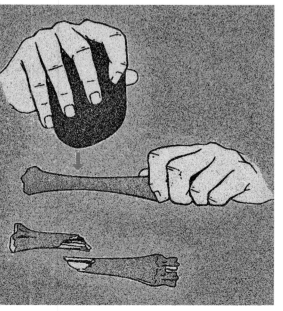

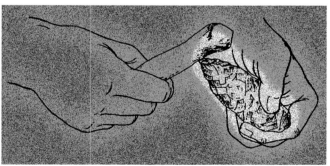

**5.** Homo erectus *worked with materials other than stone. Here we see a bone being struck to make a tool that was similar to an awl or a sharp weapon.* Homo erectus *could evaluate the potential of bone material. Using special types of chipping techniques, he was able to form a sharp and penetrating point on the bone.*

**6.** *In the workshop of* Homo erectus, *stones were also retouched with a soft hammer to refine their shape and improve their performance.*

**1.** *Hunters' campsites from 730,000 years ago have been discovered at Isernia La Pineta, Molise (Italy). These discoveries have revealed much information about the various animals of that time. The drawing shows us those that lived together and their habitats. At the bottom we see: (a) the elephant, (b) the rhinoceros, (c) the bison. The hippopotamus (d) is near the river, and on the hillside are (e) the Megaceros, (f) the fallow deer, and (g) the wild boar. Halfway up the hill is (h) the bear. High on the hill is (i) the curved-horned ram.*

# A HUNTING INCIDENT

In front of Kim's cave, a group of children are absorbed in a story that one of the elders is telling. Is it a fable? No, he is telling a story about his life and his hunting adventures. Kim draws close, greets the elder with great respect, and asks him how he feels. Foon (as he is called) has had difficulty walking ever since he had an accident during a bison hunt.

Kim asks Foon to tell the children about this mishap. And so Foon begins: "We were hunting bison that we had driven into a swamp. All of a sudden, one of them managed to come back out of the water. With his horns, he lifted me and hurled me high into the air. When I fell down, both of my legs broke. My friends carried me back to the camp. Ever since then, I could not hunt with the group. I have had to stay at home. I try to make myself useful by keeping the children company."

**3.** *The ability to use articulate speech to relate the events of the day was certainly a step ahead in the growth of human culture. The arrow points to two artistic forms of expression that are linked to language.*

**4.** *A conversation between two persons, rock painting (dating from about 4000 B.C.E.) from Jabharen, Tassili (North Africa).*

**5.** *From a fresco (dating from somewhere between 350 and 550 C.E.) in the Mayan city of Uaxactún (Guatemala): two individuals are talking.*

**2.** *The femur of* Homo erectus, *found in Java, has a protuberance (bone tumor) that may have formed after a trauma (possibly the result of a fall). This must have affected its function.*

**1. – 2.** *Burning lava running out of the volcano at Mount Etna, Sicily (Italy) and beams of light shooting up from cracks in the solidified upper layer of the lava. Volcanic activity was probably one of the acts of nature that called the attention of humans to fire. We can only imagine that, approaching with caution, a human may have "captured" the fire with some kind of instrument. In any case, this was the first victory: to catch the fire and keep it going in order to make use of it when needed.*

**3.** *Humans would then learn to build fires by rubbing hard objects, such as pieces of flint, together and producing sparks. Fire may have been discovered by accident, perhaps when some sparks ignited dry grass. After that, humans learned to deliberately and systematically build and control fires.*

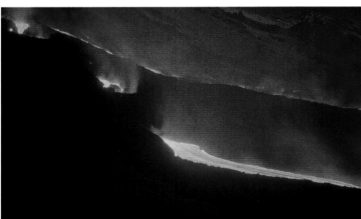

# FIRE

It is dusk. The sun is disappearing behind a hill, and Kim is walking around the huts. A woman and some children are trying to light a fire. They are striking one flint against the other while holding some dry branches. Finally, there is a spark and the dry leaves catch fire. Kim is pleased as he watches this because he knows that they have learned the technique for starting a fire. Then, while the children listen, he explains: "Fire is a friend, a powerful ally. It lights up the darkness of night. It keeps away unwanted animals, and can also help us catch animals. All we have to do is set fire to a woodland or shrubs and trees, and the animals will run out of their dens to escape. That is when it is easy to catch hares, marmots, and deer. But when we do this, we have to be armed with spears and stones, and we must do it in a group."

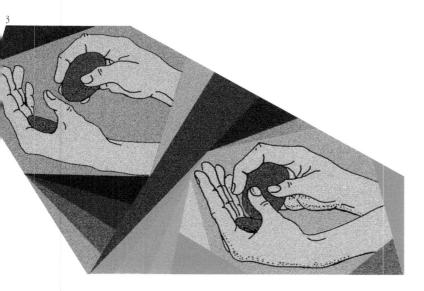

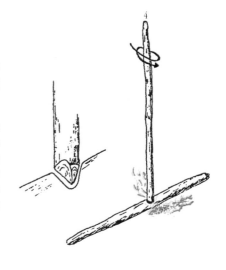

**4.** Fire could also be produced by rubbing together other substances, such as pieces of wood. Here we see one possible method: Sparks are released by rotating a stick in a hole that has been carved into another piece of wood especially for this purpose.

# DINNER

It is already dinnertime. Kim is busy cutting up pieces of meat that will be roasted, but first he has to remove the skin. He uses very sharp tools and is careful not to tear the skin, which will be used for clothing.

As the meat is roasting on the fire, the children bring fruits, berries, and vegetables that they gathered on the plain. They lay them out on the ground.

Everyone gathers in a circle: Kim, his wife, children, grandfather, and aunt. Dinner is the time when family members get together. Kim and his wife distribute the food. Everyone is hungry. Everyone sits around the fire and speaks of what happened that day.

When dinner is over, Kim and the others gather up the trash and bring it outside the camp.

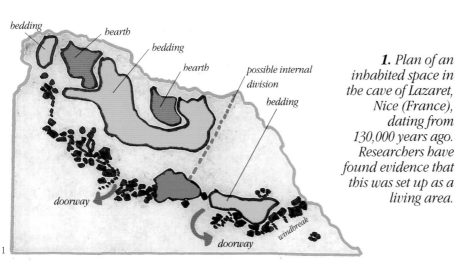

*bedding* *hearth* *bedding* *hearth* *possible internal division* *bedding* *doorway* *doorway* *windbreak*

**1.** *Plan of an inhabited space in the cave of Lazaret, Nice (France), dating from 130,000 years ago. Researchers have found evidence that this was set up as a living area.*

**2.** *Mandible of a male human (Heidelberg, Germany), one of the oldest specimens of the European* Homo erectus, *about 650,000 years old.*

**3.** *The arrow points from the picture of a mother and child to other pictures showing cultural evolution. Parents and children make us reflect upon the rhythms of nature and society.* **4.** *Front and back of a Siberian statuette of a woman, dating from 30,000 years ago. The 27 notches on the body appear to be symbols of the menstrual cycle.*

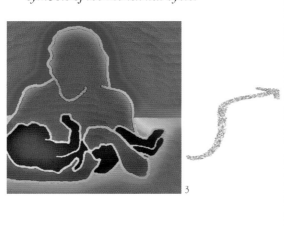

3

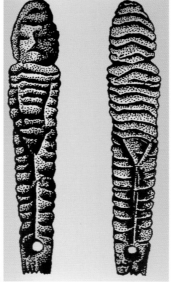

4

5

38

**5.** *A family scene in a rock painting in northeastern Brazil, from a culture that died out in 6000 B.C.E.*

**6.** *Rock engravings at Gobernador Canyon, New Mexico (U.S.), from the year 950 C.E. The picture may be of a fertility ritual. A couple are holding hands, and the woman carries a child in her womb.*

**7.** *Rock paintings frequently portrayed fertility rites. In a picture from the Navajo reservation, New Mexico (U.S.), dating from 1000 to 1500 C.E., a child on the head of a man suggests the human desire to have children.*

6                    7

# A STORM

Shadows are falling. The sky is very dark. "Those low clouds will bring rain," Kim says. "We had better stay in the cave." Just as he says this, large drops begin to fall. It is not just a passing cloud, but a real storm with thunder and lightning. All the people take cover in the cave. Sitting on the ground, they watch the downpour. Lightning lights up the valley. The rain forms thick streams that run down the valley in torrents. Lightning strikes a tree and sets it on fire.

The children are terrified and huddle close to their mother. It seems as if all of nature has let loose. "Could it be that someone in heaven wants to make himself heard? What could he want with us?" Kim wonders.

**1.** *Observing nature gave our ancestors information that made it easier for them live. In the photo, heavy rain clouds show that a storm is coming.*

**2.** *A forest fire. Trees that were struck by lightning and caught on fire were one of the natural phenomena that made humans aware of the power of fire.*

**3.** *A rainbow. The multicolored vision that appears in the sky after a storm has always been a message of peace from nature. It is one of the most popular symbols in human culture.*

## THE DAY IS OVER

The storm has passed. Parts of the camp are flooded, but the cave has offered precious shelter. Now it is night-time. Some men are speaking with Kim about their plans for the next few days, and where the group will move to next. "We can stay here a few more days, but the resources are running out," says Kim. "Not too far off in the direction where the sun rises, there is a little hill with caves in it. This might be a good place unless others are already living there. In that case, we will not disturb them. We will look for somewhere else to live."

"We could send someone on ahead to see," says one of the men. This seems like a good suggestion, and the others agree. Then they all go back to their caves to rest for the night.

Kim is still thinking about the storm, the lightning, the thunder . . . "How can nature have let loose so suddenly and frightened everyone so much? Now nature seems to want to make peace with us."

The night sky is awesome, dotted with stars. Kim looks up and thinks: "The sky is ever-changing. Some stars shine more brightly, others move and then return to their original positions. And so does the sun, every day. We are so small. Perhaps there is something larger watching over us. Perhaps our adventure does not end here in this valley."

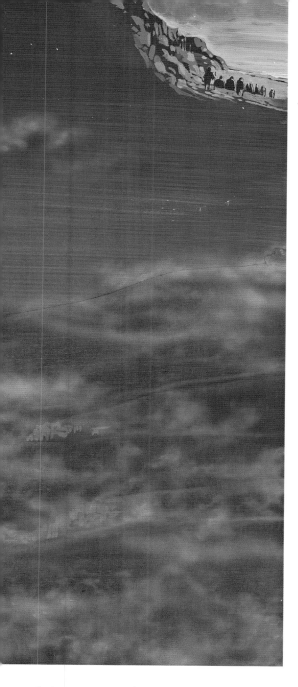

**1.** *A restoration of* Homo erectus. *By showing him in midstride, the drawing portrays him as a nomad. We know that he only stayed in one area as long as resources were available.*

**2.** *The photo shows the elements that were important to* Homo erectus *as he moved from one place to another. Most important was a body of water next to which he could set up his camp.*

**3.** *The second important element to have near a camp was abundant rock formations. They supplied stone for carving tools, and the caves and gorges in the rocks provided refuge and a place from which one could observe the surrounding area.*

# GLOSSARY

*Well-made spears with tips that were hardened by fire were invaluable to* Homo erectus *as hunting tools.*

ARTICULATE SPEECH: Language produced by a combination of fairly simple sounds. These sounds are organized in such a way that the nervous system associates a meaning with the sounds and sound combinations.

BIFACE: A stone tool, typical of Paleolithic age, in various shapes: pear, almond, heart, oval, etc. It is flaked, and eventually retouched, on both faces and along the edges.

BIPEDALISM: To walk on two legs. This is the way humans walk today. Many primates can occasionally walk on their lower limbs, but for humans, this is the only form of locomotion. Over the time, bipedalism has resulted in the lengthening of the legs and an entire series of skeletal and muscular adjustments.

BLADE: A fairly thin stone tool, made by flaking, with a length roughly equal to the double of its width.

CEREBRALIZATION: The progressive increase in brain size, accompanied by more complex function.

CHOPPER and CHOPPING TOOL: Sharp edged tools obtained by breaking off some flakes from pebbles on one or both faces.

CRANIAL CAPACITY: Volume of the braincase. It is measured in cubic centimeters.

ERECT POSTURE: Upright position of the body characterized by vertical alignment of the head with the spinal column and lower limbs. Such alignment is a necessary condition for bipedalism.

FLAKE: Roughly short and wide tool obtained from a nucleus of stone by percussion.

FLINT: Sedimentary rock formed by the accumulation of various types of deposits. It was very useful in prehistoric tool making because of its fine grain and hardness.

GLACIATION: Cold geological period characterized by vast extensions of ice in regions of the northern hemisphere.

HAMMER: Stone tool, chosen for its shape and resistance, used for creating a percussion (see also PERCUSSION).

*Death must have been a disturbing event.* Homo erectus *knew that this was something to reflect upon.*

*Exchanging news and ideas is easier as articulate speech becomes more refined.*

HOLOCENE: The geologic period following the glaciations, which encompasses the last 10,000 years.

INDUSTRY (PREHISTORIC): Items that early humans made from flint, bone, and horn that had an intentional use.

LEVALLOIS: A technique for making stone tools in which the final shape is decided beforehand by preparing a nucleus of stone. This technique was greatly used by *Homo erectus* during the Lower and Middle Paleolithic ages.

LOCOMOTION: An animal's ability to move from one place to another. The movements can vary according to the animal's organs and environment (water, land, air).

MORPHOLOGICAL: Greek word meaning "related to the form." In biological science, morphology concerns the forms of living beings ordered in a systematic classification.

NEOLITHIC: Later Stone Age, which falls between the tenth and fourth millennia B.C.E. This age witnessed the beginning of agriculture, breeding, the production of ceramics, and the first permanent villages.

NUCLEUS (or CORE): Block of stone from which many kinds of tools are made.

OLDOWAN: Culture of the Archeolithic and Lower Paleolithic eras, characterized by the presence of pebble tools (choppers and chopping tools).

PALEOLITHIC: Early Stone Age (700,000 to 10,000 years ago). Scientists divide it into three parts. The Lower Paleolithic took place from 700,000 to 120,000 years ago. The presence of *Homo erectus* covers this entire time span, but it actually begins much earlier, 1.6 million years ago, in the Archeolithic era, which is characterized by Oldowan industry (choppers and chopping tools). The Middle Paleolithic took place 120,000 to 40,000 years ago, and the Upper Paleolithic took place 40,000 to 10,000 years ago.

PERCUSSION: A strong blow with which a nucleus of stone is being hit to break off a flake. This can be done *directly* with a stone or horn hammer, or *indirectly* by putting another stone between the nucleus and the hammer, or even with *pressure* from a tool called a retoucher.

PLEISTOCENE: Period of the Quaternary era characterized by glaciations. It began 1.8 million years ago and continued until 10,000 years ago.

*Near the fire, when the group gathered for dinner, the young listened to the advice and stories of the elders.*

Homo erectus *cooperated with the other members of his group. A big hunting prey was taken inside the cave thanks to the joined efforts of three men.*

*For* Homo erectus, *animal bones were not just garbage. They were material for making tools or weapons.*

POINT: A small stone tool with a sharp end worked from splinters or blades.

QUATERNARY: Geological era that began 1.8 million years ago. It includes the Pleistocene and the Holocene periods.

REMAINS: From the Latin word meaning "found," these are objects discovered during systematic archaeological investigations.

SITE: Place where remains of prehistoric humans and their activities have been found. Such remains, discovered by scientists during a series of archeological excavations, are then passed on to the next stage of research.

TORUS: Strong protrusion of bone. The "supraorbital torus," or visor, refers to the browridge. The "occipital torus" refers to the occipital bone in the back of the skull.

*A burning shrub could provide light to keep away animals at night. Fire could also light one's way in a dark cave.*

# INDEX

# PICTURE CREDITS

*The number in boldface refers to the page and
the number in parentheses refers to the illustration.*

ANDREA BORGIA: **36** (1,2). EDITORIALE JACA BOOK (Salvador Gul'liem Arroyo): **29** (5); (Alessandro Bartolozzi): **10** (3), **27** (3 drawing), **34** (1); (Duilio Citi): **27** (3 photo), **41** (1); (Andrea Dué): **10** (2), **16** (2), **29** (4); (Giacinto Gaudenzi): **20** (1); (Jorio): **9** (3), **14** (1), **33** (4); (Ermanno Leso): **16** (1); (Renato Massa): **43** (2); (Antonio Molino): **12, 15**; (Michela Rangoni Machiavelli): **29** (3), **37** (3); (Carlo Scotti): **24** (1), **28** (2); (Roberto Simoni): **10** (4), **20** (4); (Angelo Stabin): **11** (8), **31** (2), **41** (3), **43** (3); (Fabio Terraneo): **12**. GRANATA PRESS: **41** (2). MADDALENA POCCIANTI: **22** (2).

*Illustration sources faithfully reproduced or modified*

Anati, Emmanuel. *The Imaginary Museum of Prehistory. Rock Art of the World.* Jaca Book, 2002: **27** (2), **28** (1), **35** (4), **38** (4).

Various Authors. *The Classic Maya.* Jaca Book, 1997: **35** (5).

Bonnier, Gaston, and Robert, Douin. *The Complete Illustrated Flora of France, Switzerland and Belgium in Color.* Illustrated by Julie Poinsot, Editions Belin, 1990 [Italian translation Jaca Book, 1995]: **22** (2).

Broglio, Alberto, and Janusz, Kozlowski. *Paleolithic Age.* Jaca Book, 1986: **32** (1,2), **38** (1).

Clottes, Jean, and Robert, Simonnet. "Recent Studies in a Deep Cave. The René Clastres Cave in the Pyrenees," *The Human Adventure.* Jaca Book, Year 5, no. 16, winter 1990, spring, 1991: **16** (3).

Coppens, Yves. *The Monkey, Africa and Mankind.* Arthème Fayard, 1983. [Italian translation Jaca Book , 1996]: **43** (1).

Dué Andrea, edited by. *The First Inhabited Lands. From Primates to Homo Sapiens,* vol. 1, *The Atlases of the History of Mankind.* Jaca Book, 1993: **44–45–46**.

Facchini, Fiorenzo. *Origins: Man. Introduction to Paleoanthropology.* Jaca Book, 1990: **8** (1,2, modified), **17** (5), **22** (3), **25** (7), **26** (1), **34** (2).

——— , edited by. *Paleoanthropology and Prehistory,* a volume of *The Open Thematic Encyclopedia.* Jaca Book, 1993: **10** (1,5,6), **11** (7).

Forest, Jean-Daniel. *Mesopotamia, the Invention of the State.* Jaca Book, 1996: **16** (4).

*Other pictures not mentioned here come from the Jaca Book archives.
Giorgio Bacchin is the author of those tables not mentioned here.*